SUMMARY

The Gentleman in Moscow

Book by Amor Towles

The Summary Guy

TABLE OF CONTENTS

INTRODUCTION

The Gentleman in Moscow is a novel written by Amore Towles. The novel's plot is set in the beginning of the 20th century Russian Empire and follows the story of Count Alexander Ilyich Rostov and his life in the Hotel Metropol where he has been under house arrest for thirty-two years.

The 20th century was one of the most turbulent times in the history of Europe. Old political systems were deemed obsolete. People wanted change; they wanted rights for all, not just for the wealthy. In the Russian Empire 'old and new' clashed in blood, violence, and death. During the 20th century, being noble was not very popular in Russia. Communists slowly but surely gained more and more trust from the people. Since their agenda blamed several groups of people for every misfortune that happened, being a count became very dangerous.

Alexander Ilyich Rostov knows this. He almost gets killed but is saved at the last moment in the most peculiar way.

An interesting novel, filled with historical segments, *The Gentleman in Moscow* is more than just a story of one man. It is a story of survival and uncertainty in dire times.

Mr. Summary

SUMMARY

CHAPTER 1:
THE STORY OF AN
ARISTOCRAT

The novel opens with a short description of Count Alexander Ilyich Rostov. He is an aristocrat living in Moscow in a hotel named Metropol. Rostov is perceived as a threat to the new Communist party because of two things: 1) He escaped the tsar's execution in 1918 and 2) He is a nobleman.

Being a noble was like being a priest or a capitalist. The new Communist Party did not allow anyone to be anything else besides a Communist. Because of that, Count Rostov was monitored and, after a short time, put under house arrest.

The author describes events before the Russian (Communist) Revolution occurred. He also describes Count Rostov. Alexander Ilyich Rostov is originally from Russian Nizhny Novgorod. The party becomes suspicious of him when he leaves Russia after the tsar's execution in 1918 and after he returns four years later. Count Rostov is about to be executed under suspicion for being against the Revolution but then a poem, published back in 1913, is discovered. Presumably Rostov wrote it. The poem espouses revolutionary ideas later implemented by the Communists. Because Rostov claims that he wrote it, his life is spared. He is put under house arrest in a hotel Metropol.

After being sentenced to house arrest, Rostov is then forced to move to a tiny cell. Being a nobleman, Rostov is used to living the life of luxury. But now, he must move to a tiny cell and abandon his luxurious suite.

Rostov decides to bring a picture of his late sister Helena.

The hotel looks pretty much like most luxurious American hotels. One day in the Piazza, Rostov meets a little girl. She is Ukrainian and she is nine years old. Her name is Nina Kulikova. She starts a conversation with him, asking him whether it is true that Rostov is really a count. She also wants to know whether he ever met a princess and if he ever fought in a duel. Rostov is amused by the questions of the little girl. After a short period of time, they start their friendship.

CHAPTER 2:
FRIENDSHIP WITH A NINE-YEAR-OLD GIRL

The author describes Nina's situation. Her father is a widower and is posted in Moscow for the time being. Nina is not enrolled in school, which means that she is also under house arrest. Since both of them are kept imprisoned, they decide to go on excursions throughout the hotel.

They manage to explore several rooms, such as the furnace room, the electrical room and the silver-service room. Rostov discovers that Nina has the master key for the entire hotel.

Once he returns to his cell, Rostov discovers that one of his closets was built over an old doorframe. He decides to remove the planks. Rostov discovers another room which looks identical to the room in which he is kept. He decides that he could use the second room and transforms it into a secret study.

Several days later, Rostov meets his old friend, Mikhail, nicknamed "Mishka" Fyodorovich Mindich. Rostov and Mishka have known each other since their university days in St. Petersburg.

Mishka came to the hotel in Moscow because he is attending the Russian Association of Proletariat Writers. Mishka perceives himself as a poet of the "new age" and the "art of action." The two of them reconnect and start talking about their past and their favorite subject – the philosophy of history.

CHAPTER 3:
THE REASON WHY I LEFT MOSCOW

Time passes and soon it is Christmas Eve. Rostov finds out that Nina will go away with her father for a while. She gives Rostov a present. Inside the present there is another, smaller present and inside that, there is the third, smallest present. After unwrapping the smallest present, Rostov discovers what Nina gave him: the hotel's master key.

Nina leaves with her father and time slowly passes by.

Almost a year has passed. Rostov has become accustomed to being imprisoned in the hotel. One day he meets an actress named Anna Urbanova. Anna is a seductress and it is apparent that she has an eye for the count. On one occasion, Anna invites Rostov into her room. Not long after socializing in her suite, the two of them become lovers.

At the same time that Anna and Rostov become lovers, Nina returns to Moscow and starts school.

Later at the hotel bar, Rostov meets a British aristocrat who is particularly interested in the Soviet Union. Rostov and the aristocrat start talking. During their conversation, the aristocrat wants to know why Rostov left Russia before the Revolution. Rostov explains to him that his reasons were personal and not of a political nature. The real reason why Rostov left was because a Hussar lieutenant had seduced his sister, Helena, as a form of revenge. Rostov had wooed the Hussar's girlfriend, a princess. After the Hussar seduced Helena, he slept with the girl's handmaiden. After Rostov found out about this, he shot the lieutenant. However, he shot him in shoulder and the Hussar survived. Rostov then fled to Paris and the lieutenant died in one of the battles during the Great War. While Rostov was in Paris, Helena got sick and died of scarlet fever.

CHAPTER 4:
A PART OF THE
"TRUMVIRATE"

The story jumps several years into the future. The year is 1930 and we read that Rostov has joined the Boyarsky hotel restaurant staff and that he is now part of "the Triumvirate." They run the entire hotel. With Rostov, there are two other people: Andrey, the hotel's head waiter, and Emile, the chef.

That same year, Nina returned to the hotel. She is now older and one day tells Rostov that some of her friends are going to the Kady District, the agricultural center of the Ivanovo Province, in order to collectivize it.

Rostov continues his affair with Anna. Her acting career is not as successful as it used to be. The Communists decried one of her movies because it spoke "against the Communist Party and the Revolution." Anna used to be wealthy actress, but since she cannot make any more movies, and since she is used a life of luxury, her wealth slowly melted.

The author then describes a man named Osip Ivanovich Glebnikov who comes to visit the count. Glebnikov is a former Red Army colonel and the current officer of the Communist Party. However, upon meeting with Rostov, Glebnikov admits that he is there only because he has been ordered to keep a close eye on Rostov. The count finds out that the Communists are working on diplomatic relations with several world superpowers, including France, Great Britain, and the U.S. Slowly but surely, the Soviet Union is establishing itself as the center of European manufacturing. Glebnikov wants Rostov to help him learn the languages and the cultures of the Western countries; apparently Glebnikov wants to be better diplomat. Rostov agrees. He promises Glebnikov that he will tutor him once a month.

CHAPTER 5:
TIMES CHANGE

The author then describes how things are beyond the walls of Metropol hotel. We find out that the Communists want to build power stations, steel mills, and factories. They also want to cultivate the agricultural regions. In order to do this, the Communists have to drive out those who refuse to cooperate. They are called "kulaks" or, translated into English, peasants.

But things are not exactly as the Communists hoped they would be. In 1932, a great famine killed several million peasants; the Soviet villages were almost destroyed. In order to avoid death by famine, the survivors had to migrate to the urban centers of the Soviet Union.

In 1938, Nina once again returns. Nina has married but her husband has been arrested and sentenced to five years of labor in Sevvostlag. Nina's plan is to follow him, but Nina and her husband have a daughter. Their daughter is five years old and her name is Sofia. Nina asks Rostov if he could take care of Sofia during Nina's absence. Nina promises Rostov that she will return for Sofia as soon as possible.

Mishka also returns. He is somehow distracted and later we find out that he is editing a volume of Chekhov's letters. We also find out that his senior editor has ordered him to cut a line in Chekhov's letter in which he wrote about how great Berlin's bread is. At first Mishka agrees to do what he is told, but later changes his mind. He returns to the editor's office and accuses his editor of being "too cozy with Stalin." Not long after that, Mishka is sent to Leningrad where he was questioned. In 1939, Mishka is sent to Siberia. We find out that Nina has also disappeared.

CHAPTER 6:
WHAT A BEAUTIFUL WORLD

Time jumps to 1946. The Second World War has ended and the Allies have won.

Sofia is now thirteen years old and Rostov is nearly sixty. Mishka returns to Moscow. We find out that he is in the city illegally. Mihska looks emaciated and worn down. He is researching his new project.

One day, Sofia has an accident. She falls from the service stairs and hits her forehead. Rostov immediately carries her outside, meaning that Rostov left the hotel for the first time in the last twenty years. Rostov quickly rushes to a nearby hospital. However, because of Nazi bombing and the fighting that took place in Moscow several years earlier, the hospital in in disrepair. Luckily, a surgeon comes and treats Sofia. Rostov notices Glebnikov in the hospital. He realizes that it was Glebnikov who recruited the surgeon. Because of this, Sofia makes a full recovery.

Time jumps forward. The year is 1950 and Sofia is seventeen years old. On one occasion, Rostov comes upon a young woman in the ballroom with the Piazza orchestra's conductor named Viktor Stepanovich Skadovsky. Sofia tells the count that Skadovsky is her piano instructor. The count is then amazed by Sofia's ability to play Chopin.

CHAPTER 7:
WE NEED TO ESCAPE

Two years later, Anna returns to the hotel. She is now a stage actress and decides to reside in Moscow for a while. This is something that Rostov eagerly accepts. During this time, Rostov finds out some classified information from his American comrade. Richard Vanderwhile confides in him that the Americans are worried about what could happen with the Soviet Union after Stalin's death. Vanderwhile asks Rostov to work for him as a spy, but this is something that Rostov declines. Nine months later, in 1953, Stalin dies of a stroke. A little later, Georgi Malenkov and Nikita Khrushchev take over the Communist Party.

We also find out from Katerina Litvinova, Mishka's lover, that Mishka is dead. Litvinova also presents Rostov with Mishka's manuscript, titled "Bread and Salt." Rostov admits to her that the revolutionary poem with which Rostov was credited was actually Mishka's. Rostov needed to claim authorship of the poem because he wanted to protect his friends from persecution.

The year is 1954. Sofia gets the opportunity to travel to Paris with the conservatory where she is a student. Rostov plans their emigration. First, he steals a Finnish passport from one of the hotel guests. Not long after that, Sofia departs for Paris. During the night of his planned escape, Rostov discovers a man in his secret study. This man was perceived as the enemy of Rostov: the Bishop. The Bishop discovers Rostov's goodbye letter to his friends and a map which had a route from Palais Garnier to the American embassy. However, the count succeeds in locking the Bishop in the boiler room. He knows that the staff will find him soon enough. Then, thanks to the help of Vanderwhile, all thirty telephones in the hotel begin ringing at once. Thanks to this commotion, Rostov manages to flee.

CHAPTER 8:
THE AFTERMATH

The story jumps to Paris, France. After Sofia's performance, she sneaks off to the American embassy. There, she meets up with Vanderwhile, who welcomes her. Sofia then presents Vanderwhile a book written by Montaigne. This book was a gift from the count. Upon opening the book, Vanderwhile discovers that the book has been hollowed out and filled with gold pieces.

The novel ends here.

ANALYSIS OF THE KEY CHARACTERS

Before we go the analysis of the novel, we will analyze some of the key characters and explain their role in the novel.

Count Alexander Ilyich Rostov

Count Alexander Ilyich Rostov is a good man, the protagonist of the novel, and a true gentleman. He is also an intellectual and, as such, he does not care much about politics. After the Communist Party takes over, he is wanted and his life is in danger. Rostov is sentenced to house arrest for the rest of his life in Hotel Metropol. The Communists wanted to kill him, but they decide to spare his life because of one poem. That poem had revolutionary ideas in it, something that was written in favor of the Party, so Rostov's life is spared.

Rostov is passive by nature, but regardless, he is still very critical of the Party's idealistic views of the world. Since he is highly educated and has great knowledge in history, philosophy, and literature, Rostov's point of view is that history flows in a cycle. This means that an individual can do absolutely nothing in order to change things and that the only thing he can do is make the best out of it. Rostov befriends the hotel staff and guests. By doing this, Rostov learns the hotel's business. After realizing that Sofia has the chance to leave the Soviet Union and Communism once and for all, his view of the world suddenly changes. Rostov creates their escape plan. He embraces his own version of revolutionary ideas. Because of his strong love for Sofia, Rostov finally realizes that he can alter the course of his and Sofia's history after all. He risks everything, even his life, in order to make their plan work.

Nina Kulikova

Nina is a very curious child who seems to challenge authority and the established rules. When she becomes a young adult, Nina is swept up in the Party's rush to collectivize the Soviet Union's agricultural provinces. During that time, her ability to think for herself is compromised and her passionate nature leads her to support the Communist regime uncritically. Later, the Communist Party, to which Nina gave everything, betrays her.

Mikhail "Mishka" Fyodorovich Mindich

Mishka is Rostov's old friend and an idealist. Mishka truly believes that literature can participate in the revolution of material life in the Soviet Union and that literature can help usher in the new age. As the Communist regime becomes increasingly repressive, Mishka sinks into despair. Mishka cannot face the fact that Russia's great literature, once the symbol of the country's independence, resistance, and resilience, is now reduced to Communist propaganda. Mishka, similar to Nina, is another victim of the regime. He is a tragic figure, but unlike Nina, he is aware of his flaws and he manages to embrace them.

ANALYSIS

The Gentleman in Moscow is a story about two worlds. One is the world of gentlemen, of chivalry, and of culture. The other is the world of repression, propaganda, seclusion, and isolation of minds and physical bodies.

It is not easy to live in a world where propaganda and repression rule. If a person obeys and does what the regime tells them to do and how to live, then that person will have no problems. His or her life will be spared and they will be left alone. But if a person thinks, behaves, or does anything "out of the ordinary," that person will face severe consequences. The same happens with the Count Rostov. He is an ordinary man, a gentleman from Moscow. He has to run from Russia and flee to Paris, where he hides for several years. Upon his return to Russia, Rostov finds out that things have changed. Being a gentleman and being a noble is not so desirable.

Towles did a great job in showing us the life of a secluded man in a time that did not understand nor want him. The reader can easily understand the count's perspective and can even get into 'his shoes.' The novel is turbulent, just like the 20th century. The author did an excellent job describing the life of an ordinary person, a man who lived a life in a world that didn't want him. The novel is truly rich, not only in plot but also in characters. This empowers the entire plot and the author's message. *The Gentleman in Moscow* is a novel which every reader who loves a rich story and deep characters will enjoy.

QUIZ

Welcome to our short quiz! In this quiz our readers will have the opportunity to test their knowledge about the novel. Questions are easy to answer and every answer can be found in the summary and in the quiz answers section.

Let's get started!

QUESTION 1

"The year is_____ and we read that Rostov has joined the _____ _____ hotel restaurant staff and that he is now part of _____ _____. They run the entire hotel. With Rostov, there are two other people: _____ _____, the hotel's head waiter, and Emile, _ _____ _____.

QUESTION 2

When did Sofia get the chance to go to Paris?

    a)   1954

    b)   1953

    c)   1946

d) 1931

QUESTION 3

When did Stalin die and what was the cause of his death?

a) Stalin died in 1965 and the cause of death was pneumonia.

b) Stalin died in 1953 and the cause of death was heart attack.

c) Stalin in 1953 and the cause of death was stroke.

d) None of the above.

QUESTION 4

Why did Rostov escape from Moscow at the beginning of the 20th century?

a) He escaped because he was responsible for the Communist uprising, which was destroyed by the Empire Russia.

b) Rostov escaped because of three things: first- he was not a Communist. Second- he was responsible for death of at least ten people. Third – he was a nobleman.

c) He escaped because he was a nobleman and because of something connected with his sister.

d) Nothing above.

QUESTION 5

Rostov's enemy is known by the name 'Bishop.'

TRUE   FALSE

QUESTION 6

The true author of the poem that many people thought was written by Count Rostov was in fact his friend, nicknamed 'Mishka.'

TRUE   FALSE

QUESTION 7

What was the name of the hotel in which Count Rostov was being held?

a) Metropolitan

b) Metropola

c) Hotel Boyarsky

d) Metropol

QUESTION 8

Why did Rostov stay in the hotel for so long?

a) The Count had to stay in a hotel because the hotel was the Communist headquarters. The count was in charge of spying on the guests from Western countries.

b) Rostov's mission was to spy on members of the Soviet Communist Party. Rostov worked for the Americans all along.

c) Rostov was stationed in the hotel because he was sentenced to house arrest for the rest of his life.

d) Rostov was in a hotel simply because he was also the owner of a hotel. For him, it was more convenient to stay there.

QUESTION 9

What did Nina give Rostov as a present before she left with her father for the first time?

a) Her doll.

b) her family locket.

c) The hotel's master key.

d) A letter.

QUESTION 10

What was the name of Rostov's lover and the woman who was an actress before the Revolution?

a) Her name was Ana.

b) Her name was Anna.

c) Her name was Alma.

d) Her name was not mentioned in the book.

QUIZ ANSWERS

QUESTION 1 – 1930, Boyarsky, the Triumvirate, Andrey, the chef.

QUESTION 2 – a

QUESTION 3 – c

QUESTION 4 – c

QUESTION 5 – TRUE

QUESTION 6 – TRUE

QUESTION 7 – d

QUESTION 8 – c

QUESTION 9 – c

QUESTION 10 – b

CONCLUSION

The 20th century was a rough time, not only in Europe but in the whole world. Before the wars started and before the sounds of guns could cloud the tunes of Chopin, something happened in the Russian Empire. The Communists came to power and all the people who did not agree with their propaganda and with the "Dictatorship of Proletariat" were deemed unwelcome. Many people were persecuted and even more were banished from their land. One of them was Count Alexander Ilyich Rostov.

Rostov was a simple man and a gentleman, who was unfortunate enough to live in dire and dangerous times. Even though he was not very interested in politics, politics were unfortunately interested in him. Rostov was not killed; he was put under house arrest in a hotel Metropol- a luxurious hotel in which he spent the majority of his life. But his seclusion and isolation was not boring: during the years spent in the hotel he met many people. Some of them were painful reminders from his past. Others were signs of a brighter future.

The Gentleman in Moscow is an excellent and thrilling novel written by Amor Towles. Love, passion, tragedy, sometimes pure luck and unstoppable urge: the urge to get out and to live. To live far away from bloodshed, far away from regime and from everything that prevents us from being what we are.

Thank You, and more...

Thank you for spending the time to read this book. I hope you hold a greater knowledge of *The Gentlemen in Moscow*

There are many individuals just like you who would like to learn about *The Gentlemen in Moscow.* This information can be useful for them as well so I would highly appreciate it if you post a good review on Amazon Kindle where you purchased this book and share it on social media (Facebook, Instagram, etc.)

Not only does it help me make a living, but it helps others obtain this knowledge as well. I would highly appreciate it!

www.amazon.com

We have other summary books available for you as well.

1- Summary – Wheat Belly by The Summary Guy:

https://www.amazon.com/Summary-William-Detailed-Summary-Weight-ebook/dp/B00RIE1Z5K/ref=sr_1_1?ie=UTF8&qid=1486882657&sr=8-1&keywords=the+summary+guy

2- Summary – How to Stop Worrying & Start Living

https://www.amazon.com/Summary-Worrying-Paperback-Hardcover-Audiobook-ebook/dp/B06VVKCLQ4/ref=sr_1_1?ie=UTF8&qid=1491015523&sr=8-1&keywords=the+summary+guy

3- Summary – The Giver

https://www.amazon.com/Summary-Quartet-Complete-Paperback-Audiobook-ebook/dp/B06XZPPN7V/ref=sr_1_1?ie=UTF8&qid=1491540894&sr=8-1&keywords=the+summary+guy

4- Summary - The Hard Things About Hard Things

https://www.amazon.com/Summary-Horowitz-Building-Paperback-Hardcover-ebook/dp/B06Y2WHLKM/ref=sr_1_2?ie=UTF8&qid=1491540894&sr=8-2&keywords=the+summary+guy

Thank you for taking the time to read this book, please give us a good review on Amazon to support us, so we (my team and I) can make more summaries for you!

https://www.amazon.com/s/ref=nb_sb_noss?url =search-alias=aps&field- keywords=the+summary+guy&rh=i%3Aaps,k%3 Athe+summary+guy

---

Want to learn how to think wiser and better?

Tips for building business, productivity, investing, smarter shopping, etc.

Check out our website: www.thinkingwiser.com

Facebook page: Thinking Wiser (Just Click)

Made in the USA
Middletown, DE
27 May 2017